ALL ABOUT
Dogs and Puppies

Grosset & Dunlap

For David and Doug—L.D.
For Charlotte and Isabel: We *will* get a puppy!—E.H.

Special thanks to Ellie at the Cape Code Kennel Club.

Library of Congress Cataloging-in-Publication Data

Driscoll, Laura.
    All about dogs and puppies/ by Laura Driscoll; photographs by Elizabeth Hathon.
      p. cm.—
    Summary: Describes different kinds of dogs and talks about how to choose and care for a puppy.
    1. Dogs—Juvenile literature. 2. Puppies—Juvenile literature. [1. Dogs.] I. Hathon, Elizabeth, ill. II. Title.
  III. Series: Grosset & Dunlap reading railroad book.
  SF426.5.D75   1998
  636.7—dc21   98-2911
                                                             CIP
ISBN 0-448-41841-X   2005 Printing   AC

ALL ABOUT
Dogs and Puppies

By Laura Driscoll • Photographs by Elizabeth Hathon

Grosset & Dunlap, Publishers

Can you imagine a world without dogs? It's not easy. These days dogs are just about everywhere you look! They're in homes across the country and around the world. They star in movies and TV shows. They work in real life as guard dogs and police dogs. They're even in our history books! Did you know that the first living creature to visit outer space was a dog?

Dogs and humans have been good friends for at least fourteen thousand years. That's a long time. So it's no wonder dogs make such good pets. They've had lots of practice.

Dogs come in all shapes and sizes. There are very big dogs and very small dogs. There are dogs with floppy ears and shaggy fur, dogs with pointy ears and short fur, and dogs of many different colors. It all depends on what type, or *breed*, a dog is.

Each dog breed belongs to one of seven groups.

Working dogs include breeds that work as police dogs, guard dogs, search-and-rescue dogs, and sled dogs. These important jobs call for brave, smart dogs that can recognize and obey lots of commands.

Siberian Husky

Great Dane

Rottweiler

Herding dogs can be trained to herd sheep or cattle, and to protect them from wild animals.

Border Collies

Shetland Sheepdog

Welsh Corgi

Hounds are good trackers. Some hounds use their extra-strong sense of smell to follow animals over very long distances, or to help the police find missing people.

Greyhound

Irish Wolfhound

Norwegian Elkhound

Airedale Terrier

Terriers have long been used by hunters to chase animals out of underground holes. Many terriers have a patch of long fur on their chin that looks like a little beard.

West Highland Terrier

Norfolk Terrier

Sporting dogs are used for bird hunting. Some, like setters and pointers, sniff the air and then point with their bodies to show hunters where birds are hiding nearby.

Hungarian Vizsla

English Setters

English Cocker Spaniel

Nonsporting dogs are kept mainly as pets today, even though some of them were used for hunting or herding many years ago.

Bulldog

Bichon Frise

Dalmatian

Toy dogs are the smallest breeds of all.

Yorkshire Terrier

Chihuahua

Cavalier King Charles Spaniel

All of these dogs are called *purebred* dogs. Purebred dogs are dogs whose mother and father are of the same breed. But many dogs are *mixed-breed* dogs—they are a mix of two or more breeds. A mixed-breed dog might look like its mother in some ways and its father in others.

Dogs are mammals, like we are. After a mother dog gives birth to puppies, she feeds them with milk from her body and watches to make sure each puppy gets enough.

A family of puppies born together is called a *litter*. Puppies are born with their eyes and ears sealed shut. At first, they can only feel and smell their way around. Then, about two weeks after they are born, the puppies' eyes and ears open up.

Puppies in the same litter might be different colors.
And they might be different in other ways, too.

In this litter, one puppy is very independent.

One puppy stays close to its mother.

The other puppies are very playful.

If you want to get a dog or puppy of your own, there are a few things to think about first. Like any pet, a dog is a big responsibility. It will need to be fed and walked every day, and taken to the doctor when it is sick. Will you be able to give a dog a happy, healthy, and loving home?

There are so many different kinds of dogs to choose from. Some breeds need lots of exercise. Some breeds bark more than others. Some breeds are small all their lives, while others will grow up to be almost as big as you are! So think hard about what kind of dog you want.

Where can you get a dog of your own? One place to look is the animal shelter, where there are always healthy dogs waiting for a good home. Or if you want a puppy, maybe you know someone whose dog just had puppies.

You will probably want a puppy that is between six and eight weeks old. Puppies this age are old enough to leave their mother and go to live with their own human family. Look for a playful and active puppy with clear, bright eyes and a clean, shiny coat.

Young puppies need to be fed three or four times a day in small amounts. There is special puppy food made just for them. Puppies also need lots of cool, fresh drinking water, kept out all the time in a bowl they cannot tip over.

If a puppy misbehaves, its owner must say "No!" in a stern voice. She never ever hits her dog. And when it does obey her, she rewards it with big hugs and lots of praise.

Dogs of all ages should be brushed often. But dogs should have a bath only when they really need one, because too many can dry out their skin. Some dogs love baths. Others hate them. Either way, wet dogs like to shake themselves dry—so watch out!

Time for a walk! Most dogs need at least two walks a day to stay healthy. Walks are good exercise, and dogs usually like them because it's a chance for them to see other dogs.

Just like people, dogs need to visit the doctor for a checkup about once a year. An animal doctor is called a *veterinarian*. In the waiting room at the vet's office, dog owners sit with their dogs, petting them and talking to them softly to keep them calm. Sometimes it's hard for a dog to stay calm with so many other dogs around!

Inside the exam room, the vet checks everything—from the dog's eyes and ears to its toenails and feet. The doctor also might take the dog's temperature and listen to its heartbeat.

What a healthy dog!

Dogs haven't always looked the way they do today. In fact, thousands of years ago, they looked more like wolves. Wolves and dogs are very closely related to each other. In the wild, wolves live together in groups called *packs*. In every wolf pack, there are two wolves—one male and one female—that are the leaders of the pack, and all the other wolves follow and obey them.

In some ways, dogs are still a lot like wolves. If a dog sits when its owner says "Sit!", it is because it thinks of its owner as the leader of the pack. Some dogs are happiest when they are following instructions from their owners or trainers—whether it's playing fetch with a ball, working as a search-and-rescue dog, or herding sheep.

Herding dogs are some of the hardest working and most helpful dogs around. Sheep farmers use whistles, hand signals, or voice commands to tell the dogs where they want the sheep to go. Then the dogs go to work.

The dogs in these photographs are Border collies. One Border collie can herd up to one thousand sheep on its own!

Everybody knows that Dalmatians are fire dogs. But do you know why? In the days of horse-drawn fire engines, fire departments adopted Dalmatians because of their bravery and their ability to get along with horses. Sometimes, on the way to a fire, the dogs would run along next to the horses, barking and clearing the way for the fire engine. Those days are long gone, but even today many fire departments keep Dalmatians as pets.

At dog shows, beautiful dogs compete for awards. The judges look at a dog's coloring, body shape, and size. They choose one dog of each breed to get the "Best of Breed" award. The judges also pick a "Best in Show" dog—the one that they like best of all the dogs at the show.

At this neighborhood dog show, every dog is a winner! The judges have award ribbons for the Cutest Dog, the Friendliest Dog, the Most Bashful Dog, the Most Unusual Dog, and lots more! There are enough awards so that each dog gets one, because as every dog owner knows, each dog is special in its own way.

Just like people, no two dogs are exactly alike. But most people love dogs for the same reasons.

They comfort us when we are sad.

They protect us.

They play with us.

They are family....

They are our friends.